"What a book! It's like a walk in the woods, wherein you overturn a rock and find all these tiny treasures. In Melissa Eleftherion's *Suture*, a series of erasures that examine "the abject," the speaker is "willing to let / silence / confess." Caesuras are heavy with mystery. Page space pulses with not-quite-stated knowledge that slowly reveals itself over the course of the poetic sequence. The speaker "knew a violent house." The antagonist "[is] tower & / tremble." Marriage is "blood in [a] glass of white worms." However the speaker is "a fugitive / in love with / being soft," and they are determined to stay that way, even if it requires forgiveness. Eleftherion has chosen an unusual way to tell a tale with this assemblage of poems, which just makes it all the more unforgettable."

—Jill Khoury, author of *earthwork*

"Melissa Eleftherion starts with "how we're taught / to contain / the abject" and takes us through a journey where "family / was / a/ secret war." These erasure poems depict a struggle through trauma, doubt, and worth to come out the other side "resolve[d] / to matter." *Suture* gives us a well-crafted, important narrative that will stay with us."

— David Harrison Horton, author of *Necessary*

A suture stitches a wound closed, but what is left after that wound heals—a scar? Or a memory? In this new collection, Melissa Eleftherion excavates the *Flowers in the Attic* series to tell her own story in spare, haunting poems (or …sutures") that detail the lasting trauma of a violent childhood. Full of striking images, these erasures capture the loneliness of living with a secret and how only knowing love …as a treacherous undercurrent" continues to shape the speaker. However, the speaker never gives up her search for awe and wonder, and vows to …smash the glass box" while learning how to be soft and forgive. Through these many sutures, the wound heals but is not forgotten.

—Gina Myers, author of *Works & Days*

"In her third book, Eleftherion continues their study of the relationship between self and environment. Beginning with a metaphor of ammonite sutures—the seams that form between chambers of an ammonite's spiral shell — Eleftherion follows a child's perspective as their body and mind develop, leaving traces on the page. A subtle book excavated from the young adult horror novel *Flowers in the Attic, Suture* is haunted by the pathways of trauma and growth."

—Jessica Smith, author of *How to Know the Flowers*

suture

suture

Melissa Eleftherion

Table of Contents

III.

For my Gen X sisters who read
Flowers in the Attic too young.

I.

first suture

little explosions
"under a glass bell"
how we're taught
to contain
the abject
little burst sutures
in ammonite

third suture

the

blood

time

I knew

a

violent   house

3

fifth suture

childhood   o f

scattered

clocks

contradicting

my   distress

I   saved
insecurity
for
the woods

4

suture #267

One

     cringe

        over   truth

The rule   was button

          ribbon

Down in the
birdcage

I
quivered

       A
   messy scold

suture #21

I   began

with   paper dolls

        I could vaguely

be   a boy

    Absorbed   I didn't hear a
sound

The colors refracted
                        tattooed patterns
                                    like
many-faceted jewels

I
                                pretended

        I hoped to retrieve
        wonder

suture #65

awe

      was

    old books in stacks

        phonographs

awe

      was

a dead relative

of the

    wasp waist

suture #30

dead things

shimmer   in

                      dormer windows

                  there were wings
                     soft and rotting

accumulated

                  protections

I saw
whispering, whispering
      old
                           coffins

      in a silent row.

suture #27

in the

panic

                              their flesh

            grey flint stone

            slash

emerged

                        like tonsils

writing

        coils of

           silence

suture #20

That   damned

          music box

               creaked

               moonlight
                         the shape of

          his fingers

                                   demand   ing

                                   dream

seventh suture

family

    was   a

secret war

married   t   o

television

suture #12

Sunday   was

tired

faces

        underneath

this   princess

        dress

13

and

panic

suture #35

         church

w   a   s

           a

thinning

       of the soul

ninth suture

The
          glass
life

                              I played
                              stained
                              patterns

      sharp

                                    rhymes

                              to protect

            from
            catching
         rainbows

suture #28

                              Her dark

bore holes

                         tough

               peasant bones

                                   Holes

               little flecks
                         when the sun

                         fell

suture #66

a
laced-up cage

                        suffers the
                                beautiful

The silence   of that   space

                        pretend, pretend
                                my

dirt
slithering

                curious

suture #29

Before   the last

          home

b   e   f   o   r   e

the hospital   i

longed

                    to   be

                    good

suture #31

distress

was   once

my
lonely

secret

II.

suture #287

       Free
the golden

The rose
      scar

I twin
     with affection, embarrassed

Maybe I   saved hurt

Crawling to   a safe sky
I lay on that   roof
An   angry ballet

suture #8,9

The

anger

mirror

that   arched gracefully   overhead

bloomed

an

underbelly   of

concrete

I

prepare   a

23

meal

of

gesture s

suture #275

I
         dream of

leaving

It's   complicated

To hope
To trust

I resolve
to matter

suture #28

I

     follow

     irresistible

          goals

                    Competition

             a   circus

Of

     lonely

        power

While

     we

        statues

tell

every

Desire

roses   haven't

loved

twenty-first suture

while

                                        my

lips

tend

            the whisper

I

                work

            every cent

suture #201

a royal

           mouth

a   redemption
swan

I
corrupt
the
soft
light

suture #285

<pre>
          making
                  dresses
I   tear   the   bodice

A   little-girl   scream

To   crush   the   devil

My   hollow
My   round

I
                  rot   with thought
</pre>

suture #13

        I

     disguise

 grace

    with

      my

    brain

       forked

like cold

precise

snakes

suture #33

I

      fell in soft waves

      lost

a

      fragile
          crime

I   don't have to
be a good girl

suture #307

To rise

                a

                 sin

     or

magic

           paradox

I
keep

      hope

suture #133

35

enchanted   I crawl
white daisies

                              banish
                              the light

long I burn
wild
&
holy

suture #16

I'd   heal

        but

I   was

a scathing

mountain   of

milk

suture #309

As I   go   I
change

        large
a   s   a dinosaur
I
        swallow   the   men

Dream
        as
desire

I ten   der   touch
Wanting to away
Loneliness

III.

fourth suture

39

            that night

      alive again

             the soft

     trust

suture #26

our

wrath

was

intimate

memory

I stripped off
everything

suture #10

The kind of air

with

elegant

dangling

long

moments

You are

tower &

tremble

42

to fetch
a thousand

anxieties

pulse

wide

soft

suture #159

The divine
eat
marshmallows

disarm us
with
tiny bites

suture #32

Iron

wife

Breathed

remorse

accident

ballerina

fifteenth suture

love

was

a

treacherous undercurrent

a

flare

a

fist   a   belt

often
i

adored

the
trivial

piano

nineteenth suture

how

I turned   on

clutch   and

flash

shame

so mighty

the river
seized

suture #293

We were

          still

telling
 God

A little grey bird of panic

Al   l   to survive

A sterile
     love

suture #181

We people please

whisper
but cannot trust

We vow

to smash

the glass box

suture #22

                                        shared hurt

locked us

in

I   was
      that

49

kind of   girl

afraid to

lead

just

kissing   kissing

a man for protection

suture #28

                I

applied

marriage

                                        to

welts

        tender

        gentle
          maelstrom

asking

permission.

I   wanted

           blood

in

                    my   glass

of

           white worms.

suture #8

we   are

                    a tongue

                              a

                              soft

cadence

        willing to let

silence

                    confess

suture #21

we   are

                                          the night

                                          afterward

love   a

fault

                              we

never

                                          plan

suture #163

Why
I
sound
a
morning
soft

The wind scrapes crevices
We sin g a death

suture #22

     I   marry

                                   belonging

           memory

       whip the skin off

   The   someday

                                        a

   disguise

the light

invisible

suture #73

We
                    skin
memory

        arms

          and   sobs

We
                        live

                        all the while

        dance
                        and eat
                        cheese

suture #249

I felt I'd been this grass
th i s hum
I buzzed
a fugitive
in love with
be in g
soft

suture #39

We
sit   back

            our
fur

a ripple

we

                with

                        soft

arms   forgive

suture #167

We call
to the wind
to love us
clea n

Essay on the Text

If you came of age in the late 80s, someone may have sat you down in front of a tv showing *Poltergeist* (age 8), or slipped you a copy of *Flowers in the Attic* too young (age 10). Or, if you were fortunate enough to have a teenage babysitter who became so terrified during a viewing of *Halloween* that she woke you up (age 9) to watch it with her, you too may have developed a predilection for the horror genre.

Some of the erasure poems featured here work with V.C. Andrews' *Flowers in The Attic* as a source text, a book I (oddly) read and reread as a youth. The book was a beloved (yet deeply problematic) novel passed from friend to friend in hushed voices. Its premise unfolds the incestuous Dollanganger family saga, with the central story revolving around an uncle and niece who marry & have four children. When the uncle (father) suddenly dies in a car crash, the mother is left bankrupt & returns to her wealthy parent's estate to get back in their good graces. The one caveat is that she must conceal evidence of her past marriage (her children) from the patriarch in order to earn back his trust & her inheritance.

As a middle schooler who often felt monstrous on the inside, I strongly identified with most first-person outsider protagonists, and the Dollanganger children were easily-identifiable outcasts to me back then, relegated as they were to their estranged grandparents' locked attic, where they were forced to find ways to educate & entertain themselves for years on end, subsisting on kitchen scraps and poisoned donuts. At the same time, *Flowers in the Attic* was probably the first book I read that normalized emotional labor for rape victims toward their rapists.

It can be a troubled & layered relationship, this one of readers & their books that both frighten & enlighten. At times, I have found comfort reading novels that helped me externalize my own traumatic experiences with sexual violence, and YA novels can be singularly cathartic for teens and adults. *Flowers in the Attic*, however, is not a book I'd generally recommend for those seeking healing, given its graphic scenes of rape, incest, and child abuse. Though, in the recesses of my deeply troubled existence as a book-obsessed & socially awkward neurodiverse tween, it provided some solace, and helped to validate my suspicions about those family members my gut told me to mistrust. So—all in all, reading this book at a young age helped shape my identity & loaned to me moments of resolute strength.

These erasure poems are from a series I've been working on about trauma. Erasures can be a useful form for processing trauma because it can help the writer externalize events that come up, while also building towards a catharsis. They can help one extirpate & shine a light on the dark. Erasures can also be less labor-intensive because the author is not singularly responsible for the poem that's created. It is a collaboration between the author and the existing text. The creation of an erasure poem can happen organically, through a series of associations and connections that develop between the author and the page.

With a single page from *Flowers in the Attic, Petals on the Wind,* or *My Sweet Audrina* as a backdrop or landscape for each of these erasure poems, I was able to construct very sparing poems that accrete towards a narrative. Since I had a previous relationship with the text, I was able to tap back into the young person reading and connecting with those books, and also move beyond those memories to build towards something new. Found poems can have the uncanny ability to strike at the core of the unconscious tenor of what's happening, whether in the world, the mind, or the body. I like experimenting with the treasures resonant in someone else's language. These experiments also give agency to the author to reshape or reclaim the narrative to tell a story that is hidden beneath the surface, again revealing what must be revealed.

Source Notes

Third Suture: Andrews, V.C. *Petals on the Wind*, pg. 3.
Simon and Schuster, 1982.
Fifth Suture: Andrews, V.C. *My Sweet Audrina*, pg. 5.
Simon and Schuster, 1982.
Suture #267: Andrews, V.C. *Flowers in the Attic*, pg. 267.
Simon Pulse, 2009.
Suture #21: Andrews, V.C. *My Sweet Audrina*, pg. 21.
Simon and Schuster, 1982.
Suture #65: Andrews, V.C. *Flowers in the Attic*, pg. 65.
Simon Pulse, 2009.
Suture #30: Andrews, V.C. *Flowers in the Attic*, pg. 83.
Simon Pulse, 2009.
Suture #27: Andrews, V.C. *Flowers in the Attic*, pg. 228.
Pocket Books, 1979
Suture #20: Andrews, V.C. *Flowers in the Attic*, pg. 336.
Pocket Books, 1979.
Seventh Suture: Andrews, V.C. *My Sweet Audrina*, pg. 7.
Simon and Schuster, 1982.
Suture #12: Andrews, V.C. *Petals on the Wind*, pg. 12.
Pocket Books, 1990
Suture #35: Andrews, V.C. *My Sweet Audrina*, pg. 35.
Pocket Books, 1982.
Ninth Suture: Andrews, V.C. *My Sweet Audrina*, pg. 9.
Simon and Schuster, 1982.
Suture #28: Andrews, V.C. *My Sweet Audrina*, pg. 28.
Pocket Books, 1982.

Suture #66: Andrews, V.C. *Flowers in the Attic*, pg. 66. Pocket Books, 1979.

Suture #29. Andrews, V.C. *Flowers in the Attic*, pg. 29. Simon Pulse, 2009.

Suture #31: Andrews, V.C. *Petals on the Wind*, pg. 31. Pocket Books, 1990.

Suture #287: Andrews, V.C. *Flowers in the Attic*, pg. 287. Simon Pulse, 2009.

Suture #8,9: Andrews, V.C. *Petals on the Wind*, pp. 8-9. Pocket Books, 1990.

Suture #275: Andrews, V.C. *Flowers in the Attic*, pg. 275. Simon Pulse, 2009.

Suture #28: Andrews, V.C. *Petals on the Wind*, pp. 28-29. Pocket Books, 1990.

Twenty-First Suture: Andrews, V.C. *Petals on the Wind*, pg. 21. Pocket Books, 1990.

Suture #201: Andrews, V.C. *Flowers in the Attic*, pg. 201. Simon Pulse, 2009.

Suture #285: Andrews, V.C. *Flowers in the Attic*, pg. 285. Simon Pulse, 2009.

Suture #13: Andrews, V.C. *Flowers in the Attic*, pg. 156. Pocket Books, 1979.

Suture #33: Andrews, V.C. *My Sweet Audrina*, pg. 33. Pocket Books, 1982.

Suture #307: Andrews, V.C. *Flowers in the Attic*, pg. 307. Simon Pulse, 2009.

Suture #133: Andrews, V.C. *Flowers in the Attic*, pg. 133. Simon Pulse, 2009.

Suture #16: Andrews, V.C. *Flowers in the Attic*, pg. 16.
Simon Pulse, 2009.

Suture #309: Andrews, V.C. *Flowers in the Attic*, pg. 309.
Simon Pulse, 2009.

Fourth Suture: Andrews, V.C. *Flowers in the Attic*, pg. 250.
Pocket Books, 1979.

Suture #26: Andrews, V.C. *Flowers in the Attic*, pg. 222.
Pocket Books, 1979.

Suture #10: Andrews, V.C. *Petals on the Wind*, pp. 10-11.
Pocket Books, 1990.

Suture #159: Andrews, V.C. *Flowers in the Attic*, pg. 159.
Simon Pulse, 2009.

Suture #32: Andrews, V.C. *Petals on the Wind*, pg. 32.
Pocket Books, 1990.

Fifteenth Suture: Andrews, V.C. *My Sweet Audrina*, pg.
15. Simon and Schuster, 1982.

Nineteenth Suture: Andrews, V.C. *My Sweet Audrina*, pg.
19. Simon and Schuster, 1982.

Suture #293: Andrews, V.C. *Flowers in the Attic*, pg. 293.
Simon Pulse, 2009.

Suture #181: Andrews, V.C. *Flowers in the Attic*, pg. 181.
Simon Pulse, 2009.

Suture #22: Andrews, V.C. *Petals on the Wind*, pp. 22-23.
Pocket Books, 1990.

Suture #28: Andrews, V.C. *Flowers in the Attic*, pg. 87.
Pocket Books, 1979.

Suture #8: Andrews, V.C. *Flowers in the Attic*, pg. 25.
Pocket Books, 1979.

Suture #21: Andrews, V.C. *Flowers in the Attic*, pg. 343.
Pocket Books, 1979.
Suture #163: Andrews, V.C. *Flowers in the Attic*, pg. 163.
Simon Pulse, 2009.
Suture #22: Andrews, V.C. *Flowers in the Attic*, pg. 190.
Pocket Books, 1979.
Suture #73: Andrews, V.C. *Flowers in the Attic*, pg. 73.
Simon Pulse, 2009.
Suture #249: Andrews, V.C. *Flowers in the Attic*, pg. 249.
Simon Pulse, 2009.
Suture #39: Andrews, V.C. *Flowers in the Attic*, pg. 39.
Simon Pulse, 2009.
Suture #167: Andrews, V.C. *Flowers in the Attic*, pg. 167.
Simon Pulse, 2009.

Acknowledgements

Grateful acknowledgement to the editors of the following publications in which poems from *Suture* previously appeared:

Some poems from *Suture* were included in the chapbooks *trauma suture* (above/ground press, 2020). & *abject sutures* (above/ground press, 2024)

Cul-de-Sac of Blood: "Third Suture", Essay on the Text

Dream Pop Press: "Fifth Suture", "Eleventh Suture"

Hot Pink: "Suture #8,9", "Suture #26"

Petrichor: "Suture #28"

Poetry Spotlight with Rob McLennan: "Suture 20.1", "Suture 8.1"

Rogue Agent: "Fifth Suture"

SAGINAW: "Suture #159", "Suture #167", & "Suture #249"

talking about strawberries all of the time: "Suture 13", "Suture 27"

Touch the Donkey: "Suture #73", "Suture #293", "Suture #305", & "Suture #309"

Villain Era: "Suture #285, "Suture #191", & "Suture #163"

Gratitudes

Thanks so much to Delia Tramontina for being an early reader of the manuscript that became *Suture*, and for her valuable feedback. Thank you to Jill Khoury for publishing early poems from *Suture* in *Rogue Agent*, and for her kind blurb. Thank you to Gina Myers, David Harrison Horton, and Jessica Smith for their thoughtful blurbs. Thank you to Jen Stein Hauptmann for her striking visual art that became the cover. Thank you to Adam Deutsch & Cooper Dillon Books for believing in this book.

Melissa Eleftherion (she/they) is a writer, a librarian, and a visual artist. Born & raised in Brooklyn, they are the author of four poetry collections: *field guide to autobiography* (The Operating System, 2018), *gutter rainbows* (Querencia Press, 2024), *Suture* (Cooper Dillon, 2026) & *Malocchia* (White Stag, 2026) as well as twelve chapbooks including *abject sutures* (above/ground press, 2024). Her work has been widely published & recently appeared in *Sixth Finch*, *Verse Daily*, & *DIAGRAM*. Melissa served as Poet Laureate for the City of Ukiah (2021-2024), and lives in Northern California where she manages the Ukiah Branch Library and curates the LOBA Reading Series. Recent work is available at www.apoetlibrarian.wordpress.com.